THE STORY OF
IRISH RUGBY

GERARD SIGGINS
ILLUSTRATED BY GRAHAM CORCORAN

THE O'BRIEN PRESS
DUBLIN

Contents

Origins

Rugby's origins are murky. Some say it was invented in 1823 by an English schoolboy called William Webb Ellis. His school played a version of football of over 100-a-side, with each team trying to kick the ball over a line at either end of the field. As you can imagine, it was quite packed and the ball never travelled very far.

The story goes that one day William was bored and decided to pick up the ball and run with it over the goal-line. His schoolmates were a bit annoyed, but eventually realised that it would make a good game in its own right, and they named the sport after the school they all attended in the English town of Rugby.

Interestingly, William Webb Ellis spent a couple of years as a child in Nenagh, County Tipperary. Some people claim that William got the idea for rugby from watching a game called Caid, which later evolved into Gaelic football. This seems unlikely, as William was just three years old when his family left Ireland.

The only record of a woman playing rugby anywhere in the world before 1900 was at a schools match in Enniskillen, County Fermanagh. In 1887, ten-year-old Emily Valentine joined in with her three brothers when their team, Portora Royal School, was short. She scored a try in her first game and played several more games for the school.

Rugby is just one of dozens of sports that are varieties of football. The main ones are soccer, American, Australian Rules and, in Ireland, Gaelic football. Rugby has two main varieties: Union, which is played worldwide and is 15-a-side; and League, a 13-a-side game mostly played in northern England, parts of Australia, New Zealand and France. Union also has offshoots such as Touch, Tag, Sevens and Wheelchair.

Rugby Comes To Ireland

Rugby was first played in Ireland by students at Trinity College Dublin. A club was set up in the university in 1854, which may be the oldest club of any football code anywhere in the world.

Students had brought the game over from various schools in England and the rules were very confused. There were no real competitions, as there were no other clubs to play against. One match was recorded in Trinity as 'dark hair' versus 'fair hair'.

In 1867, a young man from Limerick, Charles Burton Barrington, arrived in the college from Rugby School. He knew the rules that were used there and, with his friend Robert Morton Wall, sat down and wrote up a new set of laws for his club. They introduced positions and rules, which may seem a bit funny now: one rule said 'no hacking, as distinct from tripping, is fair'; another that 'holding and throttling is disallowed'.

Rugby grew quickly in popularity in Ireland with clubs springing up in Belfast (North of Ireland 1868, Queen's University 1869), Dublin (Wanderers 1869, Lansdowne 1873), Dungannon (1873), Carlow (1873) and Cork (University College Cork, 1874). The Irish Rugby Football Union (IRFU) was founded in 1874 by most of the above clubs as well as Bray, Portora and Monaghan.

DARK HAIR 03

FAIR HAIR 07

FAMOUS GAME – THE FIRST, V ENGLAND, KENNINGTON OVAL, 1875

Ireland's first international rugby match was against England in 1875, at the Oval in London, now a famous cricket ground. England won the 20-a-side match by two goals to nil. Ireland were captained by Trinity student George Stack, with eight club-mates also in the team. The other players came from North of Ireland (six), Wanderers (three) and one each from Windsor and Methodist Colleges, Belfast. Later that same year, Ireland played England in our first home game, also at a cricket ground – Leinster Cricket Club in Rathmines.

Playing Rugby – The Basics

After William Webb Ellis picked up the ball, it took a while for people to realise they had a brand-new sport on their hands. But the game did evolve, first in Rugby School and then beyond its walls, all over Britain and Ireland.

Until the middle of the 1800s, games were played with an inflated pig's bladder – one of the animal's internal organs – wrapped in leather and stitched together. The bladder wasn't round, so the ball was more oval in shape, although not as long as today.

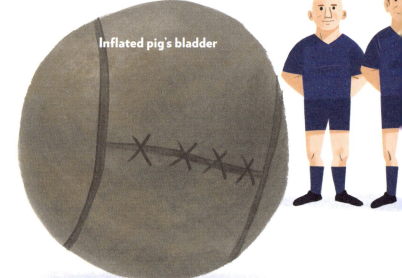

Inflated pig's bladder

Rubber bladder

Dribbling with the ball was a large element of rugby early on, although that became less important as the shape of the ball was found to be easier to handle. In 1862, rubber bladders were invented, which could be shaped more easily, helping the rugby ball to reach its egg shape. Rugby players are sometimes teased by fans of other sports as 'egg chasers'.

Leather rugby balls were notorious for soaking up water, and on wet days the ball would become much heavier. This made it harder for place kickers, trying to kick the ball over the bar from distance.

Leather rugby ball

There are 15 players on each side and a game is made up of two halves of 40 minutes. A match starts with a kick from the middle of the field and the attacking team will try to chase and capture the ball. Whoever gets possession then tries to work their way up the field to their opponents' try-line.

The referee controls the game and awards penalties against teams that break the rules. Teams can choose to kick a penalty over the bar for three points, or kick it forward into a position that gives them a better chance of scoring a try. When a player touches the ball down on or over the try-line, they score a try, worth five points.

One basic law of rugby is that the ball can only be moved forward with the hands by going backwards! If the ball is passed forward, or 'knocked on', a scrum is awarded for the other team.

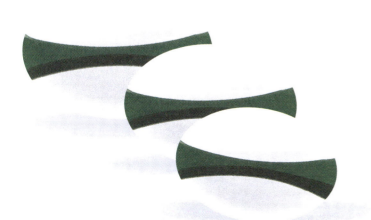

Most international games are played with balls made by Gilbert, but other ball-makers include Canterbury, Rhino and Rugbytech. Men and women play with Size 5 balls, which are 280 to 330mm long. Underage games play with Size 4 (275mm) or Size 3 (255mm).

Balls are not a precise length or girth, and vary between more rounded and more pointy ends. Rounded-end balls are easier to kick, but slower to pass; pointy ends are better for passing, but harder to kick.

9

Playing Rugby – More of the Rules

Rugby is a game for all shapes and sizes, and almost everyone can find a position that suits their physique.

The shortest adult player in modern times was French scrum-half Jacques Fouroux, known as the Little General. He was 163 cm, or 5 feet 4 inches, when he captained France to the Grand Slam in 1977, and was also manager when they later won twice.

The tallest is believed to be Scotland lock Richard Metcalfe, who towered over everyone in the line-out at 213cm, or 7 feet tall!

Ireland also had a giant player called Devin Toner, who won 70 caps between 2010 and 2020 and played more games for Leinster than anyone else. Devin is 206cm tall, or 6 feet 9 inches.

Richard Metcalfe

Devin Toner

Jacques Fouroux

Rugby was originally 20-a-side, but soon shrank to the 15-a-side game played today. The positions are now fixed, but in the early years the game was less defined. Half-backs used to have fixed areas of the field to control, so one would put the ball into the scrum on the left-hand side of the pitch, and another would do it on the other side.

Two students in Trinity College Dublin, Harry Read and Dickie Lloyd, decided to change this, with Read as the full-time scrum-half, and Lloyd the outside-half. This tactic soon became accepted everywhere.

Confusingly, teams in Australia and New Zealand sometimes use different terms for the same positions – what we call 'out-half' and 'inside centre' are called 'first five-eighth' and 'second five-eighth' down under. In the US and Canada, the Number 8 is known as '8-man'!

Other positions that are not known today were 'goaltenders', 'tends' and 'rovers'.

Rugby has always had a wacky points system, and frequent changes over the years brought it to what we have today: five points for a try, two for a conversion and three for a penalty goal or drop goal.

In 1875, scoring a try gave you a chance to 'try' to score a 'goal' by kicking the conversion. Tries on their own counted for nothing, and 'converting' the try into a goal gave the kick its name.

In the late 1880s, a point-scoring system was adopted:

Try: 1   **Conversion: 2**   **Penalty: 2**   **Drop goal: 3**

Then in 1891, the game's lawmakers changed it to:

Try: 2   **Conversion: 3**   **Penalty: 3**   **Drop goal: 4**

Two years later, they switched it to:

Try: 3   **Conversion: 2**   **Penalty: 3**   **Drop goal: 4**

In 1948, the drop goal was reduced in value:

Try: 3   **Conversion: 2**   **Penalty: 3**   **Drop goal: 3**

In 1971, it was decided to increase the value of a try:

Try: 4   **Conversion: 2**   **Penalty: 3**   **Drop goal: 3**

And again in 1992:

Try: 5   **Conversion: 2**   **Penalty: 3**   **Drop goal: 3**

It was once permitted to kick a goal from a mark, and to kick a field goal off the ground. Both of these are now illegal.

The most points ever scored in an international match was 145 by New Zealand against Japan (17) in the 1995 World Cup. Simon Culhane celebrated his debut by scoring a try and kicking 20 conversions. The All Blacks scored 21 tries, with Marc Ellis running in six of them. Australia beat Namibia 142-0 (22 tries) in the 2003 World Cup.

Ireland's highest score came in 2000, on tour in America when they beat the USA 83-3. Centre Mike Mullins scored a hat-trick of tries. The highest score ever recorded in an adult match came in 1973, when now defunct Danish club Comet beat Lindo 194-0. The most recorded in a European competition came in 2002, with English club Saracens putting Romania's Dinamo Bucharest to the sword 151-0.

The Provinces: Connacht

Connacht has usually been the weakest of the four provinces, with just 26 clubs in the five western counties, 16 of them in Galway. But they have had their moments, including sharing the Interpro title in 1956, 1957 and 1965, and their crowning glory in winning the Pro12 League in 2016.

Connacht were founded in 1885 and play their home games at the Sportsground in Galway, which holds 8129.

Aengus McMorrow **Ray McLoughlin** **Bundee Aki**

Connacht wear green-and-black shirts and green shorts, with a design using the province's crest of an eagle's head and a hand holding a sword.

The first Connacht native player to win an Irish cap was Aengus McMorrow in 1951, while the first to captain Ireland was Ray McLoughlin in 1975.

Great Connacht players to play for Ireland since include Ireland and Lions captain Ciaran Fitzgerald, Eric Elwood and John O'Driscoll, and in recent years Bundee Aki, Mack Hansen and Finlay Bealham.

John Muldoon has played 327 times for Connacht, the most of all players.

From the start, Irish rugby was organised around the four ancient provinces of Ulster, Connacht, Leinster and Munster. Men's Interprovincials were held from the 1870s, but only became an official competition in 1946 and ran until 2002. Since then, the teams play each other as part of the URC, with the winner collecting the Irish Shield. Counting all tournaments (and including shared titles), Leinster have won 35 times, Ulster 30, Munster 26 and Connacht 3. Women's Interpros started in 1999, and Munster have won 16, Leinster 6 and Ulster 2.

GLORY DAY

Connacht's finest hour came in Murrayfield in Scotland in May 2016, when they beat Leinster in the final of the Pro12 League. Under coach Pat Lam and captain John Muldoon, Connacht had won 15 of their 22 regular season games, finishing second behind Leinster. They beat Glasgow Warriors 16-11 in the semi-final to reach the Grand Final. With tries from Tiernan O'Halloran, Niyi Adeolokun and Matt Healy – his tenth of the season – they ran out 20-10 winners.

Rugby for Boys and Girls

It has never been easier for girls and boys to take up playing rugby. Almost every town in the country has a club, and almost everywhere is close to a club.

Most beginners will start with 'leprechaun rugby', from as young as six years old. This is a fast, free-flowing and exciting form of the game with little contact – you tackle an opponent by touching them. Leprechaun rugby gets players used to handling the ball and running with it. Many children start playing with RugbyTots, run by a Dublin-based company.

When players reach the age of eight, they take up mini-rugby, which is eight-a-side and played for 60 minutes. As players get older, the games become longer and include more players – U11 and U12 are 10-a-side or 12-a-side.

Girls' youth rugby is split up into three age bands: U14, U16 and U18.

There are competitions as the players get older, but most young players will play fun 'festival' rugby.

Lots of children take up rugby at secondary school, where the sport is an important part of school life. One of the oldest rugby competitions in the world is the Leinster Schools Senior Cup, which has been played for since 1887. The final is traditionally played on St Patrick's Day, 17 March. Dublin's Blackrock College has won the cup an amazing 70 times.

UNDERAGE WORLD CUPS

The youngest Ireland teams are fielded at U18 boys level, while the U20 team get to play in a World Cup every two years.

Ireland have twice been beaten in U20 World Cup finals. The 2016 team lost the final in Manchester 45-21 to hosts England. Ireland fielded several players who went on to successful careers in the sport, including internationals Andrew Porter, James Ryan, Hugo Keenan, Jimmy O'Brien, Jacob Stockdale and Max Deegan.

Ireland lost the 2023 final 50-14 to a powerful France team in Cape Town.

2016 Under 20 World Cup

Béibhinn Parsons

The youngest player ever to play for Ireland was Béibhinn Parsons, capped against the USA two weeks before her 17th birthday, in 2018. In an interview, she joked about how she had to finish her school homework the day after the match.

Béibhinn, from Ballinasloe, County Galway, got a letter from Ireland legend Ollie Campbell congratulating her and giving her three pieces of advice: 'No.1: Score tries; No.2: Score tries; No.3: Score tries.' Béibhinn took his advice and scored five tries in her first ten games for Ireland.

The youngest male to play for Ireland was Frank Hewitt, who was 17 years 157 days old on his debut against Wales in 1924.

The youngest player to play Test rugby was Semi Taupeaafe, who was 16 when he played a Test for Tonga against Western Samoa in 1989.

The Six Nations record is held by Ninian Finlay and Charles Reid, who were both pupils at Edinburgh Academy. Both played for Scotland and both were exactly 17 years 36 days old when they made their debuts, in 1875 and 1881! The Guinness Book of Records gives the record to Finlay, who had lived for one less leap year and so was one day younger.

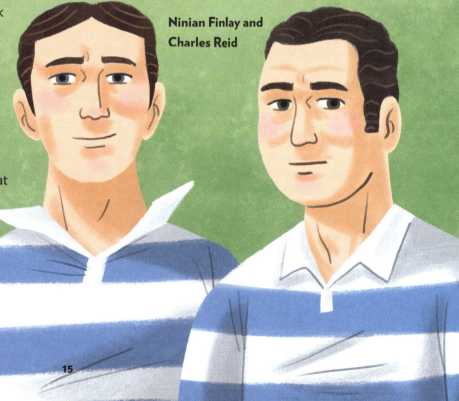

Ninian Finlay and Charles Reid

Playing For Ireland

It is a terrific honour to be picked to play for Ireland, and one shared by just 1157 men since 1875 and around 300 women since 1993. To line up to sing the anthems for the first time is always a great memory for a player.

Rugby in Ireland always ignored the border and made its own arrangements for national anthems. Up to the 1950s, Ireland used to play regularly in Belfast, usually against Wales, and before those games 'God Save The King' was played. At games in Dublin, the Irish anthem, 'Amhrán na bhFiann', was played by the army or garda bands.

But when Ireland travelled to New Zealand for the first World Cup, in 1987, the players realised that anthems would be played before games and the IRFU would not permit 'Amhrán na bhFiann'. One of the players had a tape cassette of the traditional Irish song 'The Rose of Tralee'. And that crackly, fuzzy version was the tune played in stadiums before Ireland's games.

It was 'pathetic' according to one player, while coach Mick Doyle joked at a press conference that another player was not selected because 'we couldn't be certain that he knew all the words to "The Rose of Tralee".'

For the 1995 World Cup, the IRFU commissioned songwriter Phil Coulter to write 'Ireland's Call', which has since become the anthem at all rugby internationals, and adopted by Ireland teams in hockey, cricket, rugby league and motor racing.

THE KIT

Early Ireland rugby players could not have imagined the shirts worn today. Back in the 1870s, Ireland wore woollen jerseys, which were itchy and became heavy in wet weather. The first Ireland game shows the 20 players wearing green-and-white hooped jerseys, long white pants (called knickerbockers) and long, hooped socks. Players also wore their velvet international cap!

Eventually, it was found that heavy cotton shorts were more suitable for player comfort, and by the 1890s the classic Irish green shirt with white collar and cuffs was worn, with a crest embroidered with shamrocks. That look lasted more than 100 years. These days, players wear tight-fitting modern synthetic fibres such as polyester, which last longer and let the skin breathe. But the green shirt, white shorts and green socks look is still the same!

You are said to 'win a cap' for every game you play for Ireland. Players are awarded an old-fashioned dark green velvet cap with a gold tassel on their debut, but do not actually get any more! Special caps are awarded when a player reaches 50 and 100 caps, and occasionally they are awarded one at a World Cup. Nine players have won 100 caps, and Brian O'Driscoll has won the most with 133.

GREAT PLAYER – LYNNE CANTWELL

Ireland's most capped female player is Lynne Cantwell, who won 78 caps and 8 more in Sevens tournaments. Lynne, from Swords in Dublin, only took up rugby when studying at the University of Limerick, and played the game in Ireland, England and New Zealand. She was centre on the Ireland team that won the 2013 Grand Slam and reached the semi-finals of the 2014 World Cup.

Playing For The Lions

The British and Irish Lions is a team that goes on tour every four years, either to Australia, New Zealand or South Africa. It is selected from the best players from England, Ireland, Scotland and Wales, and to be picked to go on a Lions tour is the highlight of many players' careers.

The Lions play in red shirts (for Wales), white shorts (for England) and blue socks (for Scotland) with a green turnover (for Ireland).

The tours started in 1891 as 'the British Isles team', with the name Lions not introduced until 1924. While Australia were usually beaten, tests against South Africa and New Zealand always proved difficult.

It was not until 1971 that a powerful Lions side beat the All Blacks (two tests to one, and one drawn), and three years later beat South Africa (3-0, and one drawn). The Lions have not won a series in New Zealand since, although they shared the 2017 tests 1-1, with one drawn. Even now, only 7 out of 41 tests have been won in New Zealand by the Lions.

IRISH LIONS

Some of the greatest Lions performances have had Irish players at their heart, such as the 1974 side that was captained by Willie John McBride. Since 1938, ten Irishmen have led the Lions in tests, more than any other nation. These have included Brian O'Driscoll, Paul O'Connell and Peter O'Mahony.

Paul O'Connell   **Brian O'Driscoll**   **Peter O'Mahony**

The Barbarians are a rugby team that invites players from all over the world to play. For many years, it played club teams in England and Wales, but in modern times it gets together to play international touring sides and special matches. The most famous Barbarians game took place against New Zealand in Cardiff in 1973, two years after the famous Lions win. The 'Baa-baas' picked players from the four nations and won 23-11 in a very exciting game.

Ireland first played the Barbarians in 1996, and have played them several times since in Aviva Stadium and Thomond Park. Since 2017, the Barbarians have also fielded a women's side.

The Provinces: Leinster

Leinster are one of the strongest club sides in European rugby, appearing in seven Champions Cup finals in the last 14 years. They have won the trophy four times – second only to Toulouse's six. They have also won the European Challenge Cup and eight United Rugby Championship titles since that competition began in 2001.

As the province where the capital city is situated, Leinster have always been a strong unit. There are 71 clubs in Leinster, and 75 rugby schools, all playing the game in various long-established competitions. The Provincial Towns Cup was started in 1888 and is highly prized by clubs outside Dublin, with Tullow, Enniscorthy and Kilkenny most successful in recent years. Leinster played their first game against Ulster in 1879, and only players from those two provinces played on the early Ireland teams.

Leinster wear a blue shirt with the province's ancient emblem of a golden harp. In modern times, the crest has evolved to include the harp and a rugby ball. For many years, the province played its home games at Lansdowne Road, before switching to Donnybrook (6000 capacity). Its home is now the RDS Arena (18,500) in Ballsbridge. When a big attendance is expected, the club will often switch venue to Lansdowne Road (51,700), or even Croke Park (82,000).

GLORY DAYS – 2011 CHAMPIONS CUP FINAL

Leinster first won the Champions Cup in 2009, beating Leicester Tigers, and lost the semi-final the following year to Toulouse. They beat both those clubs on the way to the 2011 final in Cardiff, where they faced Northampton Saints. At half-time they were losing 22-6, but Johnny Sexton inspired an amazing comeback, scoring two tries and 18 points in all as Leinster triumphed 33-22.

GREAT PLAYER – JOSH VAN DER FLIER

Josh's grandparents came to Wicklow from the Netherlands to open a radiator factory. Born in 1993, he first played for Leinster aged 21 and has played more than 50 times for Ireland. A strong, mobile wing forward, he played a major role in Leinster's drive to the 2022 Champions Cup final. Though Leinster lost, Josh was named European Player of the Season after that game, and later in the year he became the third Irishman to win World Rugby Player of the Year.

When England Came

One of the most famous games played in Lansdowne Road was a Five Nations fixture in 1973.

The story began a year before, when there was terrible violence in Derry and Belfast and a protest march in Dublin ended with the British Embassy being burnt down. Scotland and Wales were due to play in Lansdowne Road a few weeks later, but both unions pulled out.

Ireland had won their earlier games in Paris and Twickenham, so there was a lot of confidence that a rare Grand Slam could be achieved, but the Scots and Welsh dashed those hopes.

The Troubles continued in the north of the country, and a lot of people thought the rugby season could be disrupted again.

Some England players pulled out, but the team did travel to Dublin. They received a warm welcome, running out onto the pitch to a standing ovation. Willie John McBride held his Irish team back for a minute to allow the applause to ring out.

Ireland led 12-3 at half-time, with tries by Tom Grace and Dick Milliken. England struggled in the second half – Ireland full-back Tom Kiernan never had to touch the ball even once – and lost 18-9.

At the after-match dinner, England captain John Pullin began his speech by saying, 'We might not be any good, but at least we turned up,' to great applause.

It was a weird Five Nations tournament – every game was won by the home team, resulting in a five-way tie for the only time in the history of the championship.

The Troubles were not the only thing that cancelled Ireland matches. The world wars wiped out the seasons from 1915–19 and 1940–46, while an outbreak of the disease smallpox in Wales meant their 1962 visit to Dublin was postponed to November.

Snow has frequently stopped play, once at the very last minute in Paris in 2017, when the temperature was -5°C. An outbreak of the cattle disease foot and mouth postponed three of Ireland's games to the autumn in 2001.

And in 2020, the last round of fixtures had to be postponed for six months because of the COVID-19 pandemic.

GREAT PLAYER – WILLIE JOHN MCBRIDE

'Willie John' was a very popular second-row from Ballymena. He played for Ireland from 1962 to 1975, winning a then-record 63 caps. He always wore a thick white headband, which made him look fierce as he prowled around the field.

Willie John was also a Lions great, going on five tours. He was pack leader in 1971, when they won in New Zealand for the only time, and three years later was victorious captain in South Africa.

When the International Rugby Hall of Fame was set up in 1997, McBride was one of the first 15 men to be inducted, alongside fellow Irishmen Mike Gibson and Tony O'Reilly.

From Lansdowne to Aviva

Ireland have been playing rugby on the same ground for almost 150 years, but the stadium at Lansdowne Road in Dublin was originally built as an athletics track! A man called Henry Dunlop ran the Irish Champion Athletics Club, who usually held their events in Trinity College. But in 1872, they were told they were no longer welcome, so Dunlop found a field out in Ballsbridge beside the railway line.

Ireland had great athletes at the time and several world records were set there. Dunlop needed to keep his ground occupied, so he brought in two rugby clubs – Lansdowne and Wanderers – and also set up clubs for archery, cricket, tennis and cycling. Over the years, sports such as shooting, lacrosse, American football and baseball were also played there.

The stadium grew over the years and grandstands were erected. In 1928, a new East Stand was built on concrete stilts. To test the stand's safety, 8000 soldiers were brought in to jump up and down in it!

In 2006, the old ground was closed and demolished, and a new stadium was built on the site. Aviva Stadium opened in 2010 and is again home to the Ireland rugby and football teams. It has staged finals of the Champions Cup and Europa League.

FAMOUS GAME

Few people expected Ireland to do well in the 1982 Five Nations (Italy hadn't joined yet to make it Six). Ireland hadn't won the tournament for 33 years, and had lost all four games the year before. They changed captains, bringing in an Army captain called Ciaran Fitzgerald, who played at hooker. His team beat Wales 20-12 at Lansdowne Road and then beat England 16-15 at Twickenham, thanks to a pushover try by prop Ginger McLaughlin.

Scotland scored the only try in Dublin, but Ollie Campbell kicked six penalties and a drop goal to give Ireland a 21-12 win and the Triple Crown. A month later, Ireland's Grand Slam hopes were dashed when they lost to France in Paris.

Lansdowne Road has hosted many sports – pretty much all except the Gaelic games – but now it is just used for rugby, football and occasionally American football. Among the events staged was a cricket match between Ireland and a team of clowns, a live pigeon-shooting match and an exhibition of Cossack horse riders. Back in the 1880s, whenever the River Dodder flooded, the club hosted canoe races!

The stadium has also played host to non-sporting events, including many pop and rock concerts. Among the acts to play there were Harry Styles, Rihanna, U2, Westlife, Madonna and Lady Gaga, while a world concert of choirs was held in 1996 with 6500 singers. The ground has been used for sports days by some Dublin schools and for many years hosted the Leinster Schools Cup finals.

Other Home Grounds

While Aviva Stadium is now the home of Irish rugby, other grounds in Ireland have hosted international matches.

In fact, the very first Ireland home game was played in the Leinster Cricket Club grounds in Rathmines, a suburb to the south of Dublin city. The union wanted to hold it in Trinity College or the Phoenix Park, but decided those venues were unsuitable, as was Lansdowne Road. They rented Leinster for £10, and Trinity lent them a set of goalposts. England won by a goal and a try to nil.

In 1898, Ireland played Wales at Munster's home venue, Thomond Park. Thomond Park has hosted three more international games this century, while Leinster's home at the RDS Arena hosted Ireland v Fiji in 2009.

Ravenhill in Belfast was Ireland's second venue from 1924 to 1954, staging 15 games, mostly against Wales but including a 2007 World Cup warm-up match against Italy. Ravenhill was also the venue for the 2017 Women's World Cup final, when New Zealand beat England.

Ireland's women's team played their first home game in Ravenhill in 1994. They have since played at more than a dozen venues around the country, including Donnybrook (20 matches), Ashbourne (16), Thomond Park (7), St Mary's College (6) and UCD Bowl (6).

Ireland men also played 14 games at Croke Park between 2007 and 2010, while the stadium at Lansdowne Road was demolished and rebuilt.

FAMOUS GAME

A then-record crowd of 81,611 saw Ireland play England at Croke Park in 2007. Because of the historical background to the game – British soldiers killed 14 people at a GAA match on the ground in 1920 – there was a lot of emotion around the fixture. Irish players cried during the national anthem, but on the field they were ruthless. They hammered England 43-13, the visitors' worst-ever defeat in the Six Nations.

FAMOUS REFEREE

Former Ireland international Joy Neville from Limerick had the honour of refereeing the 2017 World Cup final at Ravenhill.

As a player, she had played in two World Cups for Ireland and was on the team that won the 2013 Grand Slam, winning 70 caps in all. She later took up refereeing and in 2017 was named World Rugby referee of the year. She has gone on to officiate in many top-level games for both men and women.

The Provinces: Munster

Our southern province has been at the heart of some of the most memorable days in Irish rugby. At the foundation of the IRFU, they were very much the poor relation to Ulster and Leinster, who dominated the selection panel, and thus the Ireland teams, for many years.

The crest was initially comprised of three castles, thought to represent the medieval lordships of three great families: the Butlers, Fitzgeralds and O'Briens. This century, the stag was added to the crest – an animal that always defends its own territory. The stag is also part of the crest of another great Munster family, the McCarthys, whose motto 'to the brave and faithful nothing is impossible' was also adopted by Munster Rugby.

There are 12 senior clubs in the province, including four each in the cities of Limerick and Cork, and Munster clubs account for more than half the winners of the All-Ireland League. The most successful teams are Shannon (nine titles) and Cork Constitution (six), while the AIL has also been won by Garryowen (three times) and Young Munster (once). There are also almost 50 junior clubs in the six counties of Munster.

At provincial level, Munster have topped the men's Interpro table 26 times, while Munster Women have won 16 out of 24 Interprovincial tournaments.

The province plays most of its home games at Thomond Park in Limerick, with occasional visits to Musgrave Park in Cork. In Europe, Munster have played 195 matches, more than any other club in the continent, winning the Champions Cup in 2006 with a powerful team led by Anthony Foley, and again two years later captained by Paul O'Connell.

GREAT PLAYER – PAUL O'CONNELL

Paul O'Connell was captain of the brilliant Munster team that won the 2008 Champions Cup final over Toulouse. Every one of the forwards – and their four replacements – were current or future internationals, including legends such as John Hayes, Jerry Flannery, Donncha O'Callaghan and man of the match Alan Quinlan. Standing tallest in the famous red shirt was O'Connell, who also captained Ireland and the Lions, winning 108 international caps. A talented lock, Paul suffered from injuries late in his career, and a torn hamstring at the 2015 World Cup meant he never played for Ireland again.

FAMOUS GAME

Very few rugby matches have inspired books, songs and even a stage play, but Munster's 12-0 victory over New Zealand in 1978 did. That All Blacks team were a powerful one – they beat England, Ireland, Scotland and Wales on the 1978–79 tour, ending with a record of 17 won, one lost.

That 'one' came in Thomond Park, Limerick, in front of a crowd of more than 12,000 people. A try from Christy Cantillon was converted by Tony Ward, and with the huge crowd cheering them on, Ward dropped a goal in each half to put Munster out of sight. Try as they might, New Zealand could not break down the province's defence and were held scoreless. Afterwards, the brilliant All Black wing Stu Wilson admitted, 'We were lucky to get nil.'

Women Rugby Pioneers

The first woman or girl known to have played rugby was Emily Valentine, in County Fermanagh back in 1887, but it took almost another century for women to play against each other without being part of men's teams.

In the 1920s, French women played in a league for a sport called 'barette', which was 12-a-side touch rugby, but the first recorded women's rugby team was at Edinburgh University in 1962. The sport was played at Irish universities in the 1980s, though the first women's clubs were formed in Ireland only in 1990.

But once women found their feet in the game, progress was swift. A union was formed in 1991, and two years later, Ireland began playing internationals.

Maybe it was a coincidence, or a silent tribute to Emily Valentine, but Ireland's first game took place on Valentine's Day 1993, in Raeburn Place, Edinburgh. It was the first international for both teams, and Scotland won 10-0. The Scots actually won the first 14 meetings between the sides, and then Ireland took over and won the next 12!

Ireland played in the first World Cup in 1994, and the Five Nations two years later. The men's and women's unions joined in 2008 and, while there have been ups and downs since, the game has continued to grow, with Triple Crowns in 2013 and 2015 and the Grand Slam in 2013.

FAMOUS GAME

Ireland started the 2013 season with a narrow 12-10 win over Wales, but they knew they could do something special when they beat England for the first time, an Alison Miller hat-trick of tries the highlight of a 25-0 victory. They won the Triple Crown, beating Scotland 30-3, and clinched the championship by beating France 15-10.

To take the first Grand Slam, they then had to beat Italy, who had won only two matches in seven full seasons.

The hosts took an early lead in rainy Milan through Veronica Schiavon's third-minute penalty. Niamh Briggs kicked a penalty soon after, but it wasn't until 11 minutes into the second half that she put Ireland in front with another kick. The Italians fought hard as the rain worsened. But Ireland fought harder, holding on for the Grand Slam on St Patrick's Day.

STAR PLAYER

Winger Alison Miller was leading try scorer in the 2013 Grand Slam season with five tries, three of them coming against England. She also scored a try in the famous win over New Zealand at the 2015 World Cup. Alison is from County Laois, where her father, Bobby, was a famous Gaelic footballer. She retired in 2019 with a record 24 tries in 47 games for her country.

Rugby's Imaginary Trophies

For many years, the two most important prizes in rugby were the Triple Crown and the Grand Slam – and there was no trophy for either!

The honour of winning the Triple Crown – the phrase was first used by *The Irish Times* in 1894 – was given to England, Ireland, Scotland or Wales if they beat all of the other three sides in the same season. Over the past 120 years, England have won it 26 times, Wales 22, Ireland 13 and Scotland 10.

From 2006, a large silver shield has been presented to the winners. This has been won six times by Ireland, four times by Wales and three times by England.

Grand Slam winners still collect an imaginary trophy, awarded to a side that wins all of its games in the Six Nations. The first winner was Wales, back in 1908, when it was just the Five Nations. England have won it 13 times, Wales 12, France 10, Ireland 4 and Scotland 3. Italy, who first played in the competition in 2000, have yet to win a Grand Slam.

Ireland's four wins came under brilliant captains – in 1948 it was Jack Kyle, in 2009 Brian O'Driscoll, in 2018 Rory Best and in 2023 Johnny Sexton.

FAMOUS PLAYER

Brian O'Driscoll is one of Ireland's greatest-ever players. He played Gaelic football as a boy, before playing rugby in the Clontarf club and at Blackrock College. He was capped by Ireland Schools and was on the Irish team that won the U19 World Championship.

He played for Ireland even before he played for Leinster and scored a hat-trick of tries against France in Paris in his first season. He was three times named Player of the Tournament in the Six Nations.

In all, he played 133 times for his country, more than anyone else, as well as eight Tests for the British and Irish Lions. As a powerful centre, he also scored the record number of tries for Ireland, 46.

Not All Black Against The All Blacks

New Zealand is the most rugby-mad nation on Earth. All the other countries that play rugby at the top level have other ball games that are more popular than rugby. In France and England, football is more widely played, while in Ireland both football and Gaelic football have more players.

New Zealand has just 5 million people, but almost every boy and girl plays rugby at school. Along with a strong tradition of success and coaching, this has made New Zealand the fiercest opponents for any side. They won the first World Cup in 1987, and have won it twice since, only once failing to reach at least the semi-finals.

Their first game was only in 1903, when they beat Australia 22-3, and ever since they have been the team to beat. The British and Irish Lions have toured there 12 times, and have won only one series, way back in 1971. The Lions have beaten New Zealand only 7 times, drawn 4 and lost 30.

Ireland first played the 'Original' All Blacks at Lansdowne Road in 1905, losing 15-0. They continued to lose to New Zealand – 27 of their first 28 meetings were defeats, with just a 10-10 draw in 1973 to cheer them.

But a stunning 40-29 win in a game staged in Soldier Field, Chicago, ended that dismal run in 2016. Tries by Jordi Murphy, CJ Stander, Conor Murray, Simon Zebo and Robbie Henshaw stunned the All Blacks, starting a much better run of games for Ireland.

Ireland have certainly turned the record around in recent years. From 2016 to the end of 2022, the sides met eight times, with Ireland winning five! They beat them twice in Aviva Stadium and in the summer of 2022, came from 1-0 down to win the series with stunning wins in Dunedin (23-12) and Wellington (32-22).

STAR PLAYER

One of the greatest of all New Zealand players was Dave Gallaher, born in County Donegal. He emigrated as a child with his family and grew up near Auckland. A brilliant back-row forward, he captained the first All Blacks touring side, known as The Originals. When he retired, he became a leading coach, but he died in the First World War, blown up by a bomb on his very first day in Belgium in 1917. His story inspired the children's book *Rugby Warrior*.

The Worldwide Game

Rugby is played all over the world, in at least 130 countries, and the sport's governing body, World Rugby, has its headquarters in Dublin.

England has the most players, 2.1 million, and the USA are next with 1.5 million. Ireland is eleventh on the list, surprisingly behind Colombia, Fiji, Canada and China.

Most of Ireland's games have been against the other Six Nations and Rugby Championship teams, but they have also played Namibia, Russia, Samoa, Zimbabwe and others, usually at World Cups.

The world is a smaller place these days, they say, and that has meant lots of players moving their homes – and loyalties – to play rugby. Ireland has a long history of emigration, so there are lots of people all over the world with Irish roots, while others have come here to work and live.

Our first rugby voyager was Jason Smyth from Westmeath. He helped found Yokohama Rugby Club in Japan, way back in 1866!

Arguably Ireland's greatest rugby export was Dave Gallaher, who left Donegal aged five in 1878, when his family sailed for a new life in New Zealand. He fought in the Boer War, and was capped by New Zealand in 1903. He went on to play 36 games for the All Blacks, later coaching the side. Killed in the First World War, he is still revered as one of New Zealand's greatest players.

Over the last 30 years, as World Rugby changed the rules, Ireland has opened its doors to players from other lands who have lived here for a number of years. Many of these have become important and popular members of the team, including Bundee Aki, James Lowe, Jamison Gibson-Park and Mack Hansen.

Bundee Aki

James Lowe

Jamison Gibson-Park

Mack Hansen

Ian McKinley played for Leinster, but in 2011 lost the sight in his left eye and had to retire. He was coaching in Italy when he started playing again, wearing special goggles. He eventually won nine caps for that country – even playing against Ireland.

AJ McGinty played rugby at school in Blackrock before moving to the USA, for whom he played at the 2015 World Cup. Others who played for the US in the last few years include Paul Mullen from the Aran Islands, John Quill (Cork), Dylan Fawsitt (Wexford) and Luke Carty (Athlone).

The Clubs: Heartbeat of the Game

There are more than 200 rugby clubs in Ireland: 23 in Connacht, 71 in Leinster, 59 in Munster and 56 in Ulster. More than 100,000 men, women, boys and girls take part in the sport every weekend in season. Each province has its own competitions, with the senior leagues and senior cups fiercely contested every year.

The All-Ireland League was first played in 1990–91. Before that, the only competition between clubs in different provinces was the Bateman Cup, played between the winners of the four senior cups. There was strong demand for matches between teams around the country, with clubs keen to measure themselves against the strongest sides elsewhere.

The AIL is divided into five divisions, with ten teams in each, who play each other at home and away – 18 matches in all for each team. The Division 1A final is played at Aviva Stadium.

Cork Constitution were the first winners of the competition, and they are the only club to have stayed in the top division every season since the League began. They have won six titles, beaten only by Limerick club Garryowen with nine.

The competition has been dominated by clubs from Munster, with 19 of the 31 titles, 13 of them between the Limerick clubs Garryowen (9), Shannon (3) and Young Munster (1). Ten titles were won by Leinster clubs: Clontarf (3), Lansdowne (3), St Mary's College (2), Terenure College (1) and Old Belvedere (1). Only two clubs from Ulster have taken the crown: Dungannon in 2001 and Ballymena in 2003.

The oldest continuously active rugby club in the world is Dublin University FC, the club for students of Trinity College Dublin. Founded in 1854, it played a major role in the establishment of rugby in Ireland, helping to draw up the rules and set up what became the IRFU. It still plays in Division 1A of the AIL. More than 160 members have gone on to play for Ireland, including Jamie Heaslip, Ryan Baird and Linda Djougang.

DU FC
1854

The oldest rugby competition in the world is claimed to be the Dublin Hospitals Cup. It has been contested since 1881 between students who train in the city's teaching hospitals, currently the Mater, St Vincent's, Beaumont, the Federated hospitals and the Veterinary Hospital. More than 90 of those who played in the Cup have gone on to play for Ireland.

Stars of the World Game

Ireland has had some magnificent players over the past 150 years, some of whom have been considered the best in the world at the time. It's a team game of course, and it is hard to compare players of the past with the present, especially as it is difficult to compare players in such varied roles as prop and winger.

World Rugby started selecting its World Player of the Year in 2001, when Ireland hooker Keith Wood was honoured. After Ireland's 2018 Grand Slam, out-half Johnny Sexton collected the award, while flanker Josh van der Flier was honoured in 2022. In the same year, Terry Kennedy won the Sevens Player of the Year.

Brian O'Driscoll was shortlisted three times, and was especially unlucky to be narrowly pipped by All Black Richie McCaw in 2009. Other Irishmen to come close over the years include Gordon D'Arcy, Jamie Heaslip and Paul O'Connell. McCaw and fellow New Zealander Dan Carter each won the award three times.

No Irish woman has won the award, but Niamh

Keith Wood

Johnny Sexton

Josh van der Flier

Terry Kennedy

Briggs (2014) and Sophie Spence (2015) made the shortlist. Amee-Leigh Murphy Crowe was shortlisted for Sevens in 2022.

One of the greatest modern women players is winger Portia Woodman. She has won two World Cups, a Sevens World Cup, an Olympic gold medal, and a Commonwealth Games gold with New Zealand. She got her name because her parents, both schoolteachers, loved Shakespeare's play 'The Merchant of Venice' with its heroine Portia.

France's powerful scrum-half Antoine Dupont is one of the best modern players, winning the Six Nations player of the tournament in 2020, 2022 and 2023, equalling Brian O'Driscoll's record. He has won a Grand Slam, a World Player of the Year award, and, with his club Toulouse, two French Top 14 titles and the European Champions Cup.

Amee-Leigh Murphy Crowe

Beauden Barrett

Portia Woodman

Sarah Hunter

Antoine Dupont

Ireland played a role in the development of two-time World Player of the Year Beauden Barrett, who has played over 100 times for the All Blacks. He came to Ireland when his dad was hired to play rugby with Athlone and manage a farm. Beauden, aged eight, learned how to play Gaelic football in St Fiach's National School in Ballinacree, County Meath. Two of his younger brothers, Scott and Jordie, have also played more than 50 times for New Zealand.

The most capped female player in the world is back-row forward Sarah Hunter, who has 141 caps for England. She has been playing for her country since 2007 and has won 12 Six Nations titles, captaining England to the Grand Slam in 2017 and 2022. She has played in four World Cup finals and was vice-captain when England won in 2014.

The Provinces: Ulster

The Ulster branch of the IRFU was founded in 1879 and since 1923, the team have played their home games at Ravenhill in Belfast – now called Kingspan Stadium – which holds 18,196. The ground hosted the 2017 Women's World Cup final.

Ulster wear white shirts and white shorts, with a black-and-red trim introduced in recent years. Their crest is based on the province's crest of a red hand. There are several stories explaining this crest's origins in mythology, most of which involve a hand covered in blood seizing a banner during battle.

Ulster have won 30 Interprovincial tournaments. In 1999, they became the first Irish side to win the European Champions Cup, beating the French side Colomiers in Lansdowne Road. Ulster have also won two Women's Interprovincial titles.

There have been many great Ulster players, including Jack Kyle, Willie John McBride, Mike Gibson, Philip Matthews, David Humphreys and Rory Best.

Jack Kyle

Willie John McBride

Rory Best

GLORY DAYS

Ulster were the first Irish team to taste European glory, in 1999. They had a tough run to the final, beating Toulouse 15-13 and Stade Français Paris 33-27, before meeting another French club, Colomiers, in the final. The game was played in Lansdowne Road, which meant tens of thousands of Ulster supporters could travel and the ground was a sea of white.

The game, unusually, was try-less, but Ulster's Simon Mason was in great form with the boot, kicking six penalties, while David Humphreys dropped a goal. Colomiers kicked two penalties, for a final score of 21-6.

GREAT PLAYER – JACOB STOCKDALE

Jacob Stockdale had a truly stunning introduction to international rugby. First capped at 21 on an Ireland summer tour, scoring on his debut against the USA, he also scored on his home debut against South Africa and twice more a fortnight later against Argentina.

His Six Nations try-scoring was amazing – in 2018 he scored two each against Italy, Scotland and Wales at Aviva Stadium, and one more at Twickenham as Ireland won the Grand Slam. This Irish record of seven tries won him the Player of the Championship award, and his great form continued into the next season. Sadly, his career became blighted by injury and lack of form and he lost his place in the team, but he has hopes of adding to his 35 caps – and 19 magical tries. Only five men have scored more for Ireland and they all played many more games.

Ireland at Women's World Cups

Sadly, there wasn't an Ireland women's team when the first World Cup was organised in Cardiff in 1991, won by the USA. But after Ireland started playing internationals in 1993, they were all set to play in the 1994 competition, staged in Scotland. Sixteen countries were entered but only 11 played – Spain pulled out very late and were replaced by a Scottish Students team.

Ireland's first World Cup match was against that student side, and they won 18-5, before losing 31-0 to France. In the quarter-finals, they were pitted against defending champions the USA, who were far too strong, winning 76-0. The Americans eventually lost the final to England.

After a system of play-offs, Ireland were ranked seventh at the 1994 World Cup, which is still their second-best performance.

The year 1998 saw Ireland lose to Australia and Kazakhstan. Four years later, they were beaten 57-0 by Canada and 22-0 by Samoa, finishing fourteenth, their lowest ranking. Since then, Ireland have finished in the top eight in every tournament they have reached, with some notable wins such as 37-0 against South Africa in 2006 and 22-12 over the USA in 2010.

The biggest win of all was beating New Zealand 17-14 in 2014, and with Pool wins over USA and

GREAT PLAYER – NIAMH BRIGGS

Niamh Briggs grew up in County Waterford, and played Gaelic football for the county. She was spotted playing tag rugby and, aged 23, was invited to train with Munster. She was soon on the Ireland team, playing at the 2010 and 2014 World Cups. She won two Six Nations titles and was a member of the first Ireland teams to defeat New Zealand, England and France. She retired with more than 50 caps and is now head coach of Munster.

44

Kazakhstan, they reached the semi-finals for the first time. There they met England, who proved too strong, running out 40-7 winners. Ireland also lost the third-place play-off, 25-18 to France.

The 2017 tournament was held in Ireland, with all the pool games staged at University College Dublin, and all the early knockouts in Queen's University Belfast. Ireland's later games, plus the semi-finals and final, were played at Kingspan Stadium in Belfast.

It wasn't a great tournament for Ireland, however, despite starting with wins over Australia and Japan. They then lost to France, Australia and Wales, to finish in eighth place. New Zealand won the tournament, beating England 41-32. The final was refereed by Joy Neville from Limerick, who had played for Ireland at the 2006 and 2010 World Cups.

Only the top seven in 2017 qualified for the next tournament, meaning Ireland had to enter a European regional qualifier. There they lost 8-7 to Spain and 20-18 to Scotland. Although they beat Italy, it was the Italians who qualified.

By finishing third in the 2024 Six Nations, Ireland qualified for the 2025 World Cup, to be held in England.

FAMOUS GAME

Ireland's finest hour came in the Paris suburb of Marcoussis in 2014, where they took on New Zealand in a pool match. The Kiwis had won the four previous World Cups and hadn't lost a World Cup game in 23 years. They were 8-0 up when Heather O'Brien scored a try, converted by Niamh Briggs, to make it 8-7 at the break. It was 11-7 soon after, but Alison Miller crossed for another try, again converted by Briggs to give Ireland a 14-11 lead. The Silver Ferns equalised with a penalty, but with ten minutes left, Briggs slotted a penalty for a famous win – the first over New Zealand by any Ireland side.

Ireland at Men's World Cups

Although Ireland have had many brilliant players and excellent teams over the past 30 years, they just never clicked at the men's Rugby World Cup. In ten attempts from 1987 to 2023, they reached quarter-finals eight times, but never went beyond that. They failed to make the last eight in 1998, losing a quarter-final play-off to Argentina, and in 2007 they went out in the pool stage, again losing to the South Americans as well as to France.

The most heartbreaking defeat came in 1991 at Lansdowne Road, when a try by flanker Gordon Hamilton gave Ireland a 18-15 lead over Australia with six minutes left to play. Victory would mean a semi-final at the same home venue against New Zealand. With two minutes left, Australia had a scrum ten metres from Ireland's try-line. The ball went out to winger David Campese – with two tries under his belt that day – but he was tackled just short of the line by Brendan Mullin. The ball went loose and Australia's Michael Lynagh dived to score for a 19-18 win.

Ireland's eight quarter-final defeats came at the hands of Australia twice, France twice, New Zealand twice, Wales and Argentina.

WEIRD FACT
Although Ireland have played 30 games at the World Cup, against 17 countries, until the 2023 tournament they had never played against England or South Africa.

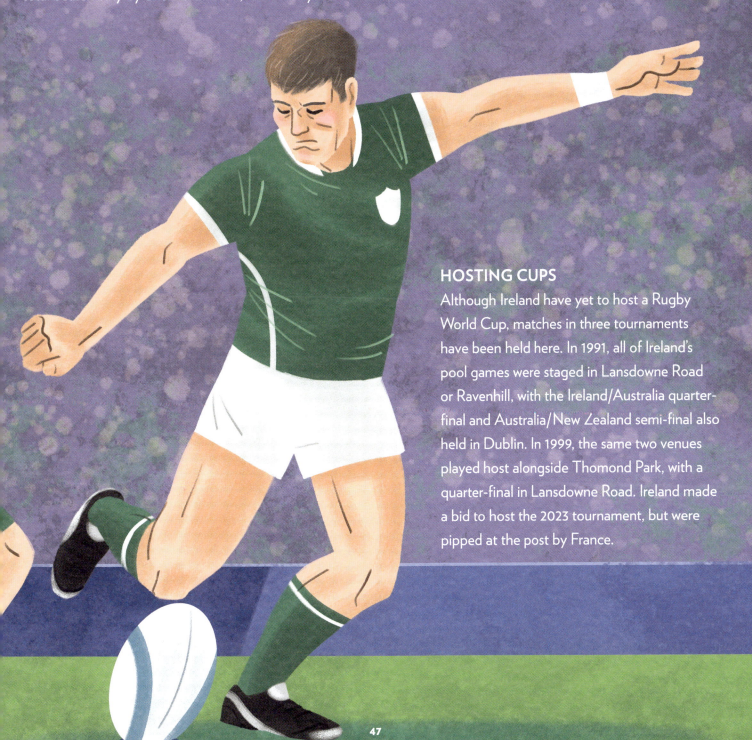

GREAT PLAYER – RONAN O'GARA

Ronan O'Gara was one of the greatest out-halves to play for Munster and Ireland. Born in San Diego in California, where his scientist father was working, he grew up in Cork, playing rugby for University College Cork and Constitution before he made his Munster debut aged 20. He played a key role in the province's two European Cup wins in 2006 and 2008.

Between 2000 and 2013, he won 113 Ireland caps, a total beaten only by Brian O'Driscoll, Cian Healy and Conor Murray. O'Gara was the first Irishman to score over 1,000 points in international matches, and in the European Champions Cup.

He played in what was probably Ireland's greatest World Cup victory, the 15-6 win over Australia in Auckland in 2011. He came on for Johnny Sexton with the score at 9-6, adding two late penalties to seal the win.

Since he retired, he has become a successful coach, winning two European Champions Cups with French club La Rochelle.

HOSTING CUPS

Although Ireland have yet to host a Rugby World Cup, matches in three tournaments have been held here. In 1991, all of Ireland's pool games were staged in Lansdowne Road or Ravenhill, with the Ireland/Australia quarter-final and Australia/New Zealand semi-final also held in Dublin. In 1999, the same two venues played host alongside Thomond Park, with a quarter-final in Lansdowne Road. Ireland made a bid to host the 2023 tournament, but were pipped at the post by France.

Gerard Siggins was born in Dublin in 1962. Initially a sports journalist, he worked for many years in the *Sunday Tribune*, where he became assistant editor. He has written several books about cricket and rugby. His *Rugby Spirit* series has sold over 65,000 copies and is hugely popular with sports-loving children around the world. Gerard regularly visits schools to talk about his books.

Graham Corcoran is an illustrator based in Dublin. He has illustrated several bestselling children's books, including the An Post Irish Book Award nominated *Dare to Dream* wriiten by Sarah Webb, and *The Story of Croke Park* written by Mícheál Ó Muircheartaigh, both published by The O'Brien Press.

First published 2024 by The O'Brien Press Ltd,
12 Terenure Road East, Rathgar, Dublin 6, D06 HD27, Ireland
Tel: +353 1 4923333; Fax: +353 1 4922777
E-mail: books@obrien.ie
Website: obrien.ie
The O'Brien Press is a member of Publishing Ireland.

ISBN: 978-1-78849-456-4

7 6 5 4 3 2 1
27 26 25 24

Printed and bound by in Poland by Białostockie Zakłady Graficzne S.A.
The paper used in this book is produced using pulp from managed forests.

Published in: